The River of Winged Dreams

The River of Winged Dreams

Poems by Aberjhani

ALSO BY ABERJHANI

I Made My Boy Out of Poetry (1997)

Encyclopedia of the Harlem Renaissance (2003)
  (with Sandra L. West)

The Wisdom of W.E.B. Du Bois (2003)

Visions of a Skylark Dressed in Black (2006)

Christmas When Music Almost Killed the World (2007)

The Harlem Renaissance Way Down South (2007)

ELEMENTAL, The Power of Illuminated Love (2008)
  (with Luther E. Vann)

The American Poet Who Went Home Again (2008)

The Bridge of Silver Wings (2009)

A CREATIVE THINKERS INTERNATIONAL
AND BLACK SKYLARK SINGING BOOK

For Bernadine Lewis and Joan Simmons, whose friendship has been like a welcoming table at which my soul has so often feasted, prayed, and breathed deeply the light that made this book possible .

"To continue one's journey in the darkness with one's footsteps guided by the illumination of remembered radiance is to know courage of a peculiar kind--the courage to demand that light continue to be light even in the surrounding darkness."
--Howard Thurman

"The mystic chords of memory, stretching from every battle-field, and patriot grave, to every living heart and hearth-stone, all over this broad land, will yet swell the chorus of the Union, when again touched, as surely they will be, by the better angels of our nature."
--Abraham Lincoln

Contents

Part II: *a halo like a world*

Part III: *earth's delights and heaven's tears*

Part IV: *The Bridge of Silver Wings*

Evolution of a Vision:
from Songs of the Angelic Gaze to The River of Winged Dreams

The notion of one powerful dream dying and another rising amidst its ashes was new to me until the life and energy of a dream that for years had empowered my creative endeavors came to an end. I was stunned because while I had accepted the reality of dreamers dying, I had never even considered the possibility that a dream itself could die. After all, it had not collapsed like a physical human body or dried up like an abused rose. It had simply gone from a recognized state of existence to an unrecognized non-existence and left me baffled in the wake of a sudden terror-filled inertia.

I accepted that the end of the dream must in some ways mean the end of me and prepared myself for whatever exactly that might mean. But although dreams are always specific to individuals they are not always respecters of persons and I found myself wrestling for a while with interpretations of a dream-informed life that was still very much in progress.

Then something which previously had eluded me became suddenly apparent: the death of a dream can in fact serve as the vehicle that endows it with new form, with reinvigorated substance, a fresh flow of ideas, and splendidly revitalized color. In short, the power of a certain kind of dream is such that death need not indicate finality at all but rather signify a metaphysical and metaphorical leap forward.

Had I not been so panicked by the notion of my beloved life-enhancing dream coming to an end, I would have realized sooner that, from the very beginning, a major part of its pattern had always been change and adaptability. It had in fact started out as a manifestation of literary visions entitled *Songs of the Angelic Gaze*, so named because in a season of visions of angels (during the summer of 2006) I found myself transcribing what I saw into short and long chains of poetry. At one point there came an image in which I stood with my father looking at a bridge teeming with angels—this sighting produced two editions of a book called *The Bridge of Silver Wings*. The second edition included works on ancestors, the newly-elected President of the United States Barack Obama, and a new suite of angel-inspired stanzas. Just as this second edition was titled *The Bridge of Silver Wings 2009*, I was fully prepared to produce a 2010 edition when the noted evolution occurred and the book now titled *The River of Winged Dreams* was born.

Four major poem additions to *The River of Dreams* set it apart from its predecessors: "Sounds Scribbled Mixed-Media Platinum"; "Notes for an Elegy in the Key of Michael (I)"; "Notes for an Elegy in the Key of Michael (II)"; and the title poem. Each of these stands out in its own right and light. "Sounds Scribbled Mixed-Media Platinum" was written during a sound painting performance, featuring Savannah's Creative

Force Artists Collective and jazzman saxophonist Jody Espina, at the Jepson Center for the Arts. My purpose for attending the event was to write a news article about it but as the painters and sculptors created their extraordinary works, while Espina and his ensemble exploded jazz throughout the atrium of the Jepson Center, my pen insisted on dancing to their creative beat and the poem wrote itself in the space intended for my notes.

The two "Elegies in the Key of Michael" are among the most surprising additions to the book, first because of the unexpected death of the great Michael Jackson in June 2009, and because of the haiku-influenced form assumed by the elegies. The title poem arrived to announce the possibility I had failed to acknowledge: that built within the conclusion of a certain kind of dream were the beginnings of another capable of simultaneously redefining and extending the previous dream. It could even be that the whole purpose of the construction of *The Bridge of Silver Wings* was to provide a path leading to *The River of Winged Dreams*, or to serve as a resting place until the river's deeper and truer nature revealed itself.

Once that deeper more true nature became clear, I had to smile at the perfect sense it made. A river is nearly the ultimate symbol for the very essence of change itself. It flows unceasingly from one point of being to another, yet continuously occupies the same bed or pathway, and accommodates life's endings with the same musical grace with which it accommodates life's beginnings, along with all the muted and explosive moments that surface between the two extremes. The gift of this awareness did two wonderful things: the first was that it confirmed my growing conviction about the power of a given dream. The second was that it extended, magnified, and clarified those *Songs of the Angelic Gaze* that first enchanted readers, listeners, and this author with the bold brilliance of their strength and the cool shimmer of their unsettling humility.

Aberjhani
Savannah, Georgia
20 January, 2010

Deliverance in Action

Between the hopelessness of despair capable of destroying a life, and the strength that comes with self assurance capable of empowering a life, there sits a great chasm with which many people struggle when attempting to cross from one side to the other. For some, the struggle occurs only once in their lifetime and, if they manage to achieve victory, their triumph endows them with a sense of confidence, inspiration, and conviction that serves their needs for the rest of their lives. For others, crossing the gulf between desolation and faith can take the form of a battle that they wage on an annual basis. For millions more—possibly your next door neighbor, a favorite grocery store clerk, your pastor, or yourself— the battle explodes into a raging war which they are forced to fight every day.

How do we make our way out of the pit of freezing shadows that can stall a life in progress upon learning one has contracted an irreversible disease? How does a spouse or parent make his or her way back to sanity after receiving the mind-crippling news that someone who "meant everything in the world to me" has been killed in a desert thousands of miles away, or on the college campus just down the street? By what means can one hope to reestablish individual balance or wholeness after suffering heart-crushing trauma at the hands of a stranger who himself is stumbling blind through grief and rage and confusion?

The truth is we do not always know how we go from falling off the edge of one cliff to running with determination beside the ledge of another. *The Bridge of Silver Wings* is what I've come to call the unknowable unquantifiable process of deliverance in action. It is what saves a given soul when that soul no longer has any idea how to save itself. It may be described as Creator, divinity, the angelic, love, good fortune, dharma, grace, faith, or any number of ways that provide hints but no irrefutably definitive explanation. It arrives when there's no logical reason to believe it shall and provides not only a sense of salvation but one of transformation. Whereas the conditions of a specific life may not undergo any kind of miraculous change, the manner in which a person perceives and addresses those issues do. With a revised awareness of what is required to bring balance, healing, hope, and prosperity back into one's life, a person is often able to achieve exactly that.

The journey across *The Bridge of Silver Wings* can be extremely frightening. At the same time, it can be filled with the kind of joyful revelations and thrilling affirmations of one's self and destiny that are experienced only when one dares to take it.

in midnight's orchard
roses blossom

Angel of Hope's Persistent Flight

I.
Wreaths of nuclear ash
decorate civilian hearts
with unresolved blood.

Greed, crowned emperor,
rules the earth with cold disdain
for harmony's path.

War poisons the land
like diseased minds downloaded
into bowls of tears.

Chaos, loving none
so much as itself, slurps and
spits dead souls like bones.

What is belief now?
What is faith that will not die?
What news from heaven?

II.
In midnight's orchard
roses blossom the secrets
that heal daylight's wounds.

Beats of broken hearts
flow waves of revelation--
open gates to strength.

Cradled in scorched arms,
a soldier's moon keeps its vows--
shines persistent hope.

This love that God is
curves in figure eights greater
than both time and space.

Death wins nothing here,
gnawing wings that amputate--
then spread, lift up, fly.

Angel of Mercy

How wickedly scars
decorate your face with strange
notions of beauty.

Your tears are muscles,
hinged on wings lunar and solar.
Your touch: life and death.

Best to meet you in
dreams from a poet's pen...than
judgments belched in hell.

In a world gushing
blood day and night, you never
stop mopping up pain.

Soothing the lips of
babes starved in Darfur. Easing
battlefield passage.

How do you fly so
softly...with such heavy loads
of sorrow and hate?

Somehow sensuous--
this sweet warm sizzle of souls
needing you so much.

Truly addictive--
whirling through forgiveness like
psalms through David's heart.

Only God singing
this song of you...makes true light
...somehow possible.

All Night in Savannah the Wind Wrote Poetry

Anxious and ancient scratches tore the air
with fingers eager to have their say,
pulling me out of bed, they cast and re-cast
nets of lexicons deep inside the womb
of the river's roaring belly, hauling up myths
born in Georgia and legends sung in Carolina,
the wind howled visions that burned the night.

Wind of April 15, 2007, screeching like knives on fire.
Wind of April 16, 2007, in Virginia 33 counted dead.

Across the wide shoulders of Tybee Island
with thumbnails of exploding waves the wind
typed furiously remembrances of Buddha;
on the aching spines of weeping pines it carved
the bleeding parables of Christ and
and the pleading hadiths of Muhammad,
oh the wind dreamed a dream that haunted the night.

Winds of the moon coughing lunar dust in my face.
Winds of the sun preaching flame down my throat.

What could it be using for ink I wondered,
and opened my window to yell--

"What are you using for ink?!"

A whirlwind of neon alphabets split the dark
wide open and inside its bright fury I saw

one-legged pirates dancing with blind prophets,
I saw kings counting gold and queens telling God.

Wind of dead flowers starving for roots.
Wind of nuclear cockroaches gobbling insanity.

Like a Passover Poet gliding from house to house
and from trembling soul to trembling soul
the wind scribbled sonnets of first time love
and weeping haikus of last hours on earth.
Up and down Broughton Street birds splattered
half-rhymes against windows and over rooftops,
the wind boomed sorrows that raged all night.

Wind of Confederate blood boiling gray miseries.
Wind of black slaves dancing juju jazz charisma.

Snatching me through the window a mighty fist
of air held me and a thousand more upside down
shook our bones like a tambourine of lightning,
wind and thunder and bones rattling cadence
for the sun that had set and the one about to rise,
for hearts pumping life and those about to stop,
the wind wrote a bloodbath too foul to read.

Wind of April 15, 2007, screeching like knives on fire.
Wind of April 16, 2007, in Virginia 33 counted dead.

The Poet-Angels Who Came to Dinner

1.
Neither had been invited but both were welcomed.
They spoke through wordless intuition, cool nods of
"Peace-Be-Still," and, "As-Goes-Love-So-Goes-Life."

Their quiet burned my brain with inklings of wonders
to come--as I set my table with what I had:
half of a cheese sandwich left over from a lucky day.

2.
From the eyes of one, my meager offering drew
liquid letters and symbols that splashed into goblets
until they overflowed with flavors of wine.

The second stranger laughed. As he howled, their
sorrow and their joy set my table anew — laid it heavy
with glazed yams, marinated dreams, and aromatic
    breads.

3.
Then their wings spread and revealed feathers painted
with the names and words of poets known and unknown.
Echoes of vows and prayers exploded
    blinding songs of light.

By the time I could see again, my guests had gone.
I stared at the bountiful table they left, too stuffed
with awe, to feast on the generosity of their grace.

4.
A knock at the door made me think they'd returned.
It was instead an old grandfather, homeless, with three
children whose parents had been lost to war and
disregard.

They had not been invited but all were welcomed.
I nodded through tears of wordless intuition:
"Peace-Be-Still," and, "As-Goes-Love-So-Goes-Life."

Angel of War

This jig death dances
around your tongue, scorns and rapes
Earth as it pleases.

Why do we shout the names of gods but worship you?

Before the first stone
crushed the first skull, fear had claimed
the first victory.

Does the potential for peace make the reality of hate sweeter?

Before the first spear,
arrow, or cannon--humans
abandoned their souls.

The phrase "nihilistic techno-bitch"--means what, exactly, to you?

Wings of centuries
flutter chaos through children's
bones, dreams, screams, and blood.

Do invitations to slaughter beauty ever make you cry?

Feathers of bullets,
feathers of daggers, missiles,
heroes, and coffins.

If missiles are faux dildos, what are babies splattered by bombs?

A halo of ice
drips the chilling truth--of this
horror mankind does.

In which countries should patriotism renounce itself first?

Were you a poet,
how easily nations would
still your howling scythe.

*If with all your power you kissed the angel of love, what then
might happen?*

Gobbler of prophets
and history's excrement,
must you never rest?

A Modest Proposal on Alternative Obsessions

Death and destruction came last year and they will be here
ill-mannered, drunk, and stinking tomorrow so with your
soul right now kiss me to a naked cinder full of un-silent
love and grappling, I promise you nations will continue
reloading guns and rehearsing stupidity tirelessly so
therefore, and thus and such, in what we call the meantime
please allow me to peruse the poetry of your velvet belly
in a very non-intellectual pre-postmodern intimate sort of
way, I want to if I may hear your heart whisper with wet
intentions to my heart things we neither know nor believe
but give strength to this embrace, it comes to me on good
authority (I swear) that supplies of ignominy and scandal
are plentiful for next week's headlines, so in this hour
wrap the starry night of my mind around your hips and
dance bare-breasted in the midnight sweetness of who and
what we are together revising history in all the ways that
matter most, I tell you this with sincerity--we can type
obituaries all day long or we can pluck nipples like guitars
and make the kind of music that life sings best.

Angel of Healing: for the Living, the Dying, and the Praying

1.
As you bury flesh--
honor spirit, savor hope,
cherish memory.

Consider heaven
as a world-weary stranger
asleep in your heart.

Quote words that affirm
all men and women are your
brothers and sisters.

Pull the child away
from feeding at the mule's tail.
Give the baby food.

2.
Compassion crowns the soul with its truest victory.
Hearts rebuilt from hope resurrect dreams killed by
   hate.
Souls reconstructed with faith transform agony into
   peace.
Wisdom applied internally corrects ignorance lived
   externally.

3.
Dare to love yourself
as if you were a rainbow
with gold at both ends.

Write a soft poem
to one you called bitch, shit head,
nigger, fag, white trash.

Live certain days dressed
in your lover's smiling soul
while she, he, wears yours.

Imagine your mind
wings intent on expanding
and watch your joy soar.

Promises of Now

Broken! The damn of covenants and souls,
of rules, egos, and love's voice shouting
through history and promises of now
dripping shadows of blood
over truth-and-flesh crimes of blood.

Broken! This vial which held Founding
Fathers' dreams broken, Whitman's
American Vista--broken--the strangled heart
of the son of man, dear God so broken,
the will to respect freedom or hope--
alas, all these tears boiling in graves.

Broken! The crystal moons of once
upon a time brotherhood and sisterhood.
(Is it safe to write this poem with its
soft black eyes reflecting faith sabotaged?)
BROken, the long wide wings He gave
brken us such a long, brokn, time, brkn, ago.

Angel of Peace

Such are these places
where lovers of bliss behold
the angel of peace:

Above the burning,
and below the cold of all
the sad killing fields;

Where poetry sighs,
smiling magic in the lap
of flesh and blood joy;

Upon the shoulders
of elders carved beautiful
by sage artistry;

Where a starbright gown
trails healing through gardens of
eternity's laughter;

In the arms of dreams
that shepherd hope through the eyes
of praying children;

Under waterfalls
bristling silk storms from the shores
of my skin to yours;

In the touch of a
woman glowing firemilk through
the tips of her breasts;

Afloat on rhythms
of minds too stoned on love to
recall how bombs work;

At the edge of a
man's kiss casting holy spells
of sweet compassion;

Inside the beauty
of faith's unburied treasure
sparkling truth and hope;

Beneath trees of song
heavy with angelic light,
evergreen with strength;

Upon the wings of

nightingales trilling comfort
to embattled grace;

In your heart's whisper,
soft as love, that *truly all
is well with your soul.*

Angel of Remembrance:
Candles for September 11, 2001

1.

B.C.: With his brother's blood wet on his hands,
Cain ran vomiting future sorrows of man.

Petals of gold cloud
swirled bright eternal letters
too soon forgotten.

2575-2467 B.C.: Immersed in themes of an unfolding story,
Egypt's Fourth Dynasty blazed pyramids of glory.

Before time or space,
Possibility's Great Heart
sang creation's birth.

April 23, 1564: Undaunted by her agony and tears,
Mary Arden gave birth to William Shakespeare.

A new sun and moon
shined pathways of choice leading
to hate, love, death, life.

April 5, 1614: Following love's beacon through the night,
Matoaka and Rolfe married peace to red and white.

History dressed up
in the glow of love's kiss turned
grief into beauty.

2.
March 10, 1913: After putting slavery and democracy to the
test,
Harriet Tubman claimed a well-earned rest.

The stink of human
blood clotting the soul's nostrils
is less impressive.

February 4, 1968: "I just want to leave a committed life behind,"
said Martin Luther King, Jr., sharing visions with the blind.

Where humanity
sowed faith, hope, and unity,
joy's garden blossomed.

July 20, 1969: "...One giant leap for mankind," said Neil
Armstrong,
living a miracle, for which many had strived hard and long.

Where ignorance shat,
violence and horror fed
the beasts of chaos.

September 11, 2001: Citizens of the U.S., besieged by terror's
sting,
rose up, weeping glory, as if on eagles' wings.

As yet, within men,
women, and children--pathways
of choice still remain.

© Fifth Anniversary of 9/11

There upon a Bough of Hope and Audacity
(In Honor of the Inauguration of Barack Obama
as the 44th President of the United States)

Songbird of speckled feathers and new millennium eyes,
you trill notes of democratic vistas heavy with light.
Chords of miraculous notions enrich your blessed voice
with strength to sing dreams into deeds well done.

Above your head Sallie Hemings' children laugh rainbows.

You are neither Christ nor King nor Lincoln.
But what you are is willing, capable, and sincere,
there upon a bough of hope and audacity
as branded by history as any have ever been.

Knights of global tables toast the lyrics of your vision.

A grand son of two continents, your heart marches
to the glorious world beat of universal drummers,
and your American dream dutifully follows: one step
for peace, another for justice, two more for strength.

Harriet Tubman's tears splash prayers for your success.

From where you perch, the trade winds of destiny
lift your songs like leaves of silken prophecies,
scattering the soft true gold of their melodies and joy:
to their rhythm a world sways, hums, and dares to believe.

Notes for an Elegy in the Key of Michael (I)

"This world we live in is the dance of the Creator.
Dancers come and go in the twinkling of an eye
but the dance lives on."
--Michael Jackson, from *The Dance*

The black star zooms gold.
Wings of white flame torch his throat.
His voice has arrived.

A nest of brothers
and sisters...mother...father
cradle your dream's tears.

First comes time, then change--
kissed into a sweet stupor
by lips of glazed song.

This magic is love
that spins your style platinum
and your soul brilliant.

A horn of plenty
spills from your hands into the
starved lives of millions.

22

Thus shines your genius,
and nations' hearts sing loud in
the key of Michael.

Like bright gleaming spells
lighting Saturn's fabled rings
you flashed classic moves.

Xenophobia--
you banished with a moonwalk...
danced hate into joy.

Tears freed your rhythm
and showered the earth's dry tongue
with dazzling sweetness.

Who can say goodbye
to the muse of an era
born to outshine stars...

Notes for an Elegy in the Key of Michael (II)

"And the dream we were conceived in
will reveal a joyful face,
and the world we once believed in
will shine again in grace."
--Michael Jackson, from *Heal the World*

Your lungs must have been
two harps for the way they flowed
music through your skin.

a halo like a world

Photographed Light of My Grandmother's Soul

The black and white photo shows you seated
in a wooden chair on the porch of a cabin
built likely by slaves, later inhabited by you:

Black American Woman Elsie Mary Bell Griffin.

One side of the image is shadowed
like the memories, the love, and perseverance
that shape your face into a hymn of quiet dignity.

The planks of the cabin's wall are straight.
Like the rows of crops you used to hoe.
The window a rectangle of inked mysteries.

From a western corner of the late summer sky
light streams brilliant wonder into the picture,
rushing through leaves to kiss your head and arms.

Thus your eternal spirit confirms your weary blue bones.

Nowhere in the photo do we see the chopped-off
heads of snakes you later fed to the hogs.
Their writhing corpses explain the heavy boots
    that shelter your feet.

The news this year is a black man in the white house.
Perhaps when alive you shook his hand in a prophetic
    dream.
Your tears bled yesterday sealed the victory claimed today.

The light somehow is like a gentle jealous god
come to claim you solely for its own. The strength
of your calm gives you the power to surrender
    everything.

Bright rapture flows and you whisper,
    "Blessed be my Lord."
Radiance splits your heart and your soul explodes
    three new stars.
Death rattles the tin roof and you command,
    "Peace, be still."

Poem Found Running Naked through
a Southern Rock Garden

Brother Julius when last we met
you had peed in your pants,
a very good thing you said
for reality's smell woke you up
to greater golden possibilities
within your here-and-now lifetime.

In your arms a poem struggled
to breathe and speak and cry.
I marveled at the sight of an "0"
bouncing off the alley wall
and the "X" stuck like two razors
between your frostbitten eyes.

You sang arias about returning to school
for a certificate of some kind,
said you loved your sons raised by me
and one day would figure out
what the hell that means, you got drunk
and kissed cocaine spit all over my face.

Scarred hands flailed among scattered letters
like seagulls dipping in and out of ocean haze.
A long heavy hiss of whimpering quatrains
drooped absurdity across your forearms as if
they had died suddenly for unknown sins.

On Mama's grave you swore

that God is good then you struck me
with an empty gin bottle and took
thirty dollars out of my laughing wallet.
I suspect my skull at this moment still leaks
. the raped tears of your strangled rhymes.

An Angel for New Orleans

O' echoes of marching saints
drum loud your songs of healing.

The improvised wings
of your feathered blue notes and neon blood
spread wide now
like the sacred myth
and swaggering hips
of your heart pulsing reserves of strength
through traumatized veins.

Holy jazzmen of small mystic hours
blow ye furious the rainbow of hope.

French Quarter of elegant mystique, Monica Blache,
Canal Street, Gustave Brother to My Visions,
Super Dome battered humble,
Jerry Bolton and Mississippi and Alabama,
beloved kins-people of Nordette Adams,
abused children all of the wind-goddess Katrina,
from our souls to your spirits
a halo like a world to embrace your trembling.

Sons and daughters of the Christ fire burning,
burn a perfect peace precisely where you stand.

O' Tap-dance Kings of Better Days,
O' Gospel Queens of Prophetic Ways,
Princes of Tears and Princesses of Prayers,

feel these weeping arms lifting your arms,
feel these raging hearts beating inside your hearts,
welcome this hope-filled breath to increase your
    breath,
feel these determined legs carrying your legs.

Scent and shadow of a bitch's brew fade like lies rescinded.
Light of angelic eyes: shine faith, speak compassion,
    bring love.

Philosophy of the Midnight Skylark
in a Jazz Suite Mode

Hot rumbling notions of bittersweet blueswomen
fog elegant sidewalks with the ghosts of tears
howling saxophonic testimonies to lies
told on history--and blame placed on love.

Street lamps and big cats wear my face gently
like a mask of painted poems and nude prayers.
In a midnight skylark jazz suite mode
the downbeat climbs its way back up to clarity.

Perfumed adagios of purple lull twilight to sleep
as rivers of winged reflections wake the power of
      dreams.
Feather and bone unravel while tongues of song
spit overloaded gigabytes of pain exploding faith.

Stoned lions roar nuclear lyrics about the way
it used to be never coming back again. Tough shit so
truly uncool. In a midnight skylark jazz suite mode
piano sorcerers translate prophecies of angst
into silk equations of bebop equals mc/square
      sublime.

Sounds Scribbled Mixed-Media Platinum
at the Jepson Center 3/22/09
(regarding Jody Espina and
the Creative Force Artist Collective)

A man sitting monkey-like
on the rooftop of his brain
calculating the precision
with which sunbeams
seduce moonlight
is only as spectacular maybe
as a river passably scatting
red-wine imitations of Louis or Ella.

But a man leaning un-harnessed
over the blue-diamond cliffs
of his jazz-baptized soul
as he weaves southern adagios
and spur-of-the-moment riffs
into new millennium bebop Mozart suites
makes for a different order of musical flora:
worthy of sonic revelations painted abstract divine.

Such a human being, one observes,
takes to the air on his saxophone
as though it were Pegasus
even as his legacy-blessed hands
channel light through the golden womb
of an artist's lexicon
conducting pantomimes of creative bliss,

signaling xylophonic spectrums of possibility unlimited.

He ripples like Low Country marsh grass--
and painters smear genius
upon canvases of parallel motion.
His heart pounds his fists with fire--
and keyboards rendezvous naked with strings
and percussions that amplify passion's brilliant voice.
His eyes explode poems--
and sculptors mold lightning into tangible vision.

A man sitting monkey-like
on the rooftop of his brain
is due the applause such feats earn him.
But a man leaning un-harnessed
over the blue-diamond cliffs
of his jazz-baptized soul
maybe deserves an angel-guarded pyramid or two--
layered with platinum and stuffed with gold.

Sunday Afternoon and the Jazz Angel Cometh

One arm is a crystal-blue saxophone,
the other a platinum-feathered keyboard —
yours is the music that colors our dreams.

Sunday afternoon and the jazz angel cometh
tap-dancing philosophies of the drum-roll
over a bebop-stay-cool bridge of silver wings.

As history bleeds forbidden light
thunder-heavy tears drip flavored adagios,
splash and explode into champagne solos.

The sacred mystery of improvisation
is hatred's final aesthetic reconciliation
to the fact of love shining forever supreme.

Your skin is human-hued and tiger-striped.
Your software likes the contradiction.
At the edge of madness you howl diamonds
    and pearls.

Broken-hearted volcanoes sob your rhythms
as midnight flowers blossom your blues and
between their fingers prophets snap lightning
    to the beat.

In the center of time's thorny labyrinth there you
are--naked you swallow quasars and spit raw genius,

cook your poems fresh, make music, make sense,
make life.

Once Was a Singer for God
(remembering Nekia)

1.

Once you were a singer for God--
yes, you, who within your mother's womb
dodged the hooks and poison sent
to eclipse your light before it shined;
who, abandoned in a field of serpents
clapped hands to the hissing of fanged omens.

Born in a year of misbegotten moons,
Louie the good mad angel found you too late.
Already blackened by the high noon sun,
already diseased by rejection,
one hand reaching for the world you'd left,
one grabbing for a stranger's lonely tit.

On the island of Daufuskie you mistook
the smell of dead crabs for that of roses.
How you stuffed your mouth with the psalms
steamed and served by a grandmother's tears--
ignoring the whip that broke your back,
and the ridicule that gutted your heart.

2.

An outrageous instinct to love and be loved
blinded your arms to lines of propriety--
Women and Men, Christians and Jews,
Muslims and Buddhists, white, black, red, brown.

An outrageous instinct to love and be loved
executed your brain every hour on the hour.

3.
No one knew how you transformed
scars on your back into scented songs
pleasing to a church's nostrils. Or how
the imprisonment of your son
and the murder of your daughter
coated your tongue with heaven's favor.

Brother was that you screaming like a wheel
burning inside a wheel, watching the stars
of your fate reconfigure a chosen destiny
into crimson midnights of tragedy?
Was that your mind running naked through the West
while your soul warbled haikus in the East?

Once you were a singer for God--
who baritoned superbly life's incongruities
until 72 years old you sat on concrete steps
humming, "what the world needs now"--Is what?

The gun in your mouth was nothing like a song,
your exploded skull one jacked up finale.

Angel of Friendship's Enduring Faith

"Over and above us there's then the angel playing."
--Rainer Maria Rilke, *Duino Elegies* (No. 4)

I.
The lights of friendship
shapeshift from tears of jade pearl
to hearts of diamond.

This way of being
is a kind of love that seeks
no fear or evil.

Like the soft twinship
of sisters in Texas spinning
faith out of silk words.

This way of being
peers deep inside beginnings to
safeguard their endings.

Like Tiger Lily
blooming scented prophecies
of soul's song burning.

II.
In a world made of
battlefields, the dreams we live
too often are slain.

*My brother's journey
in part is my own, therefore
I sing it in peace.*

The halo of trust
by its nature is fragile —
effort gives it strength.

*My sister's journey
in part is my own, therefore
I sing it with hope.*

Blessed be true friends
in our lives--for with them we
inherit true joy.

A Poet's Birthday Dance through
Fire and Rain

Lighting her pipe and puffing her years,
Grandma Elsie said, "When I was a girl
God showed me my whole life. Scared me.
Didn't know what I was seein' 'til
all that time filled up like a fat man's belly.
Now I know. Breaks my heart. Makes me so happy."

Her gin and coffee voice wraps around me
like a cashmere scarf of spring and autumn.
I recall four innocent eggs from a pigeon's nest
crashing at my guilty feet. Grandma was that
God revealing the fate of the two sons
and twin daughters I would never know?

Childhood was a slippery diving board
on which often my heart cracked, bouncing,
splashing, into piranha-hosted orgies.
Thrill of being noticed so intoxicating
that I didn't mind being eaten alive.
The more my life bled, the louder it laughed.

At night words sneaked into my bed--
triple-sexed pronouns slurped my virginity.
My gypsy dreams spurted liquid ballads and
perfumed sonnets. A lexicon of hunger stained
fevered sheets with sticky genius and marijuana
   tears.

In daylight I tended carefully my garden of
darkness singing secret terrors to the earth.
Thus did language authorize my fear
to dismiss itself--and knowledge empower
my body to act with passionate wisdom.
Out of muddy turds flew freedomsongs of mystic blue.

Slouching towards manhood I dragged with me
a world as well as my dick but mostly--
a heart addicted to the scent of dreams,
arms libertarian in their will to embrace,
a soul eager to bear the sins of Love,
a mind unafraid to waltz naked in fire or rain.

Angel of Earth Days and Seasons

A soft dream of green
colors starlit intentions
with sincerity.

In your hands winter
is a book with cloud pages
that snow pearls of love.

Your flight shines classic--
composed of symphonic nights
and honey-hued days.

Inside your laughter
spring's kiss animates the beat
of summer's warm song.

In your hair oceans
leap with sky-blue abandon
and sacred timelines.

Eyes of bright autumn
stare with red tear-stained wisdom
at human regret.

Bombs explode gashes
that flicker tales of men's blood
splattering your lips.

Rivers of poets
flow blues-heavy urgencies
naked on your knees.

Even when muddy
your wings sparkle bright wonders
that heal broken worlds.

In the dancing fields
of your sweet and holy ways
heaven blossoms gold.

A Poet's Birthday Dance through
Fire and Rain 2007

Stripping off my clothes with his wings
Louie the good mad angel said,
"Sure as flies go hog-crazy over poop,
death does love itself a bona fide poet."
Then he shut my bewildered eyes and twice spun me
around inside the piano poems of Duke Ellington.
Opening my eyes, I saw a mountain of frozen night--
"This is the grief that will rule your early years."
I then saw acres of wheat flooded with honey-colored
brilliance pouring like gold from another world--
"This is the sweet that will color the sky as it flows
from agony to grace and fills your latter years."

In a skin tapestry of northern lights and
strawberry fields, a woman and I wore
each other's soul like twin coats of mink starlight.
We smoked the legends of sacred intimacy
without regard to mortal boundaries.
We danced the prophecy of twilight moaning in
   tongues.
Love taught me to die with dignity
that I might come forth anew in splendor.
Born once of flesh, then again of fire,
I was reborn a third time to the sound of
my name humming haikus in heaven's mouth.
And destiny kissed me hard 'til I trembled seed.
And vision played me--like a shepherd's hollow
   reed.

With lips of shadow and tongue of soft storms,
the good mad angel whispered my footsteps
through barb-wire corridors of screeching hell.
How did we tango so well to the bitter cackles
of junkie jackals hooked on the sorrows of others?

Bright spirits of my children wing my heels
with solar flares of gnosis, and cosmic songs of bliss.
My father's soul cloaks my shoulders with endurance.
My mother's prayers build diamond bridges to the
    future.
I step in flame, turn west--spin above water and fly
    east,
the dance of rain cleansing, the music of fire
    exploding.

earth's delights and heaven's tears

Angel of Grace

Her heart strums the voice
of her maker--His will the
only song grace knows.

As humans explode
destruction, her feathers shine
sweet resurrection.

An arc of ages
unborn and untold, describes
this numinous flight.

An adoration
for mercy trembles rainbows
blinking through her eyes.

The stars where her wings
sing, pulse silver poetries
of faith undying.

Ezekiel at his
wheel spins a spell of healing.
Weeps a dawn of hope.

This light burns as true
here on Earth as in Heaven.
Rose lips shine "Amen."

The River of Winged Dreams

I.

None of us know from where the others,
or even ourselves, have come.
Only that we are nakedly here,
shivering on the river's bleeding banks,
looking the slaughtered way we do:
The woman dressed in blood-spotted zebra-skin
with a mouth drooling from her forehead;
a man with volcanoes erupting
serpents of flame out of his face.
And halfling children, only part human,
and part something else: like half starving dogs,
or half dead fish, or half withered roses.
On both sides of the river we stand.
Ignore eyes staring up from the red mud.
Twirling waves of violet and turquoise
sing the stories of our crimes and virtues.
We ache God's burning mystery the way Earth
aches human beauty damned by human hatred.
On both sides of the river we stand.
Souls as dead as Goliath's lopped off head.
All of us long past dying,
and rarely, if ever, prone to crying.
The light shining miles beneath the waves
itches our tongues with vicious hunger.

II.

Each roll and wave of the river
Flashes a new song and a new color.

Light rises at midnight from the water's bottom
like a giant angel of pulsing stars.
It shines a language known to one soul
and one soul only, singing the solitary story
of that woman, that man, or halfling child.

It calls them from the hissing mud of the trembling shore
into the womb of water and gleaming death.
And that is when it happens--
A glowing circle of winged dreams rises
 from the water, surrounds the fallen soul
in a ring of time and destiny confirmed:

dreams of heaven painted upon the earth,
dreams of desert winds embraced by rainforest desires,
dreams of earthquakes calming their epileptic rage
to the heartbeats of orphaned infants...
A bridge of silver wings stretches
from the dead ashes of an unforgiving nightmare
to the jeweled vision of a life started anew.
Two unicorns of morning light stride forward
as One Robed In Exploding Stars peels back the night.
Between the receding dark and sudden brilliance,
the dead recall their names and scream prayers
for the soul lifted beyond the waves.

III.

As stained shadows return, so does waiting--
for the dance of fire that devours grief,
for memories of the life that love used to bring,
for the healing language of the river of winged dreams,
for one dead dreamer to breathe light again.

54

A Coat and Shoes for Halloween

Watching his reflection waver
on heat waves of the old man's soul,
the young man sweated poison and said,
"I'm naked old dawg, give me your coat!"

Twice around the sun like an ancient notion
the old man sailed his wisdom,
then farted a lightning bolt and prayed,

"In the days when hyenas of hate suckle
the babes of men, and jackals of hypocrisy pimp
their mother's broken hearts, may children
not look to demons of ignorance for hope."

The young man's snot-slimy hands pumped
a trigger--click, BOOM, click, BOOM,
click, BOOM, click, BOOM, four times.
Ejaculating a stream of dead fleas, he said,
"I'm sorry old dawg, I need your shoes too."

Running, dressed in untied boots and a
flapping coat, he fell over a ten-year-old girl.
Her seven-inch knife slit his confusion
as she yelled, "Man you scared me with all
that funky stink comin' out your heart!"

Watching his reflection weep
in the mirror of the old man's soul,

the young man listened as the old man prayed,

"In the days when hyenas of hate suckle
the babes of men, and jackals of hypocrisy pimp
their mothers' broken hearts, may children
not look to demons of ignorance for hope."

Angel of Christmas Love Shining Bright

I.
Sweet, this elixir
of eternity's passion
commanding my glide.

Soft, this explosion
from alpha to omega
sizzling our names raw.

Here is the timeless
mystery that pays no heed
to death's greedy pride.

Songs of hearts divine,
mortal, angelic, holy,
billow starlit wings.

Here are lips of flame
eager to be extinguished
by love's liquid sigh.

II.
The ancient story
tells itself anew, dressed in
syllables of now.

Hope flexes and soars--
through eyes welcoming newborns
to earth's green legend,

through scarred tongues singing
battlefield fare-thee-wells for
comrades gone to peace.

Addicted to bliss,
dark heaven floods the soul
bright with miracles.

Stars wishing upon
the potential of humans
shine faithfully on.

Tybee Island Love Storm

Timid blue waves of oceanic chords
flood the cavern of our silence with echoes
of ballads our sighs and skin once taught
an envious diamond-studded dawn.

I weep for the twilight when your starlit heat
destroyed the chains of my hungry desperation.
Make me again: what your dream said I was--
a coconut-heavy island on fire with mysteries of you.

All around our hearts, hurricanes howl
reminders of slaughtered intimacies.
Lightning blazes poetry of hope nearly damned.
Thunder rocks joy to a song of love reborn.

The Christmas Angel Who
Whispered My Name

You spoke... and the laws of physics rebelled.

Blessings upon the heart, you lavishly bestowed
like songs of morning glories perfuming the dawn.

You spoke and glaciers of hidden memories melted.

My addiction to sorrow, you patiently soothed
with sweet oils of wisdom and healing herbs of faith.

An island of lost identity broke the ocean's ragged surface.

My lust for kindness, you satisfied with
chocolate diamond lips of champagne and poetry.

A rose larger than a mountain boomed thunder and love.

In the valley of the shadow of broken worlds
your wings dazzled and light reclaimed its beautiful
    power.

You spoke and trees wet with prayers glittered peace
    beneath the sun.

As the love in your eyes sang softly my name,
the rhythm of your flight resurrected my own.

A Friend Like a Drunk Poem
on New Year's Eve

"The air is filled with strangely human
birds."--Guillaume Apollinaire,
from *The New Spirit and the Poets*

1.
Your wife calls. Asks me to take your keys,
make you stay here tonight. She refuses
your refusal to leave the world to its chosen pains.

Long ago I stopped trying to convince you
that your hands are not roadside bombs.
Your tears not rapists. Your arms not starving
    children.

2.
You say you feel like a woman who can't stop giving
    birth.
Like a man just discovering he is worthy of love.
Like heat surfing dream-waves of burning cosmic
    intention.

I consider how the syllables of your soul have never
hung my imperfections from a gallows of public
scrutiny while wallowing in the gigglings of neurotic
    tapeworms.

3.

Your lines style splendor in cashmere meters.
Your rhymes pulse quasars of quantum compassion.
There is no sacred love your pen will not kiss, pray
for, or heal.

Forty-eight thousand friends subscribe to your blog
on MySpace.
They are witty with you, get horny too, and
sometimes sublime.
But know nothing of the nightmares you puke on my
shoes.

4.

At midnight your wife calls again. Says Happy
New Year
and she will still love you sometime tomorrow
after lunch.
Tells me I am not a bad poet and an even better
friend.

At the end of "Auld Lang Syne" you open more
champagne.
I take a hard deep breath to scold you for your
weakness.
We hiccup at the same time, and hum in harmony
as if on cue.

Angel of Valentine Days and Nights

"Love is what we were born with. Fear is what we learned
here." –Marianne Williamson,
A Return to Love

Now come the whispers
bearing bouquets of moonbeams
and sunlight tremblings.

Un-winged and naked,
sorrow surrenders its crown
to a throne called grace.

Two minds buried deep
in torment, lift up their heads
toward hills of faith.

In an age of bombs
guzzling blood, skylarks merge peace
with thought and action.

Songbirds of the grave
arise to the pulse and glow
of a new lyric.

Two frostbitten hearts
melt the ice binding their touch —
trust in life again.

Spiritual lights
and sensual flame brew sweet
mysterious heat.

One wing of midnight
and another of shy dawn
soar through twilight daze.

Two rivers splash joy
in burning communion with
their private delight.

The power to fly
crackles wild inside twin needs
to welcome love home.

The Comforter on Your Bed

"Let me have no face or name for you,
So that being the thief I may give you
more."
--Yves Bonnefoy, *Two Boats*

Grows soft acres of acrylic snapdragons
fenced in by stitches of silken lines
from Solomon's song to a queen born of legend.

In midnight's light it resembles a painted screen
with platinum streams of poetry flowing moonlit
sweetness
between the parted breasts of jeweled mountains.

In the bright of dawn it thickens like a quilt.
With patches of burnt flags, faded moans,
silhouettes of kisses, and blood-stained prayers.

Scented memories of humid summer sighs...
and gently thawed whispers in winter,
mingle hope and fire in a silent curious gaze.

This is what our love is--a sacred pattern
of unbroken unity sewn flawlessly invisible inside
all other images, thoughts, smells, and sounds.

This comforter on your bed adores the way the beat

of your heart demands all of his heat and attention,
as if he were made of mink lined with a sunrise--

and you a naked dreamer feasting on warmth.

Poets of the Angels

Feet sandaled with dreams
tread paths of vision leading
to wisdom's sharp peaks.

On a bridge spanning
earth's delights and heaven's tears
jeweled throats shine psalms.

Stars ink your fingers
with a lexicon of flame
blazing rare knowledge.

Hurricanes grow calm
for the pleasure of hearing
your souls' hidden rhymes.

You are the hybrids
of golden worlds and ages
splendidly conceived.

To accommodate
humanity's whims, gore floods
your cleanest pages.

In obedience
to eternity's beauty
prayers cloak your heart.

Your pain is a school
unto itself--and your joy
a lovely temple.

Syllables gathered
on the shores of your genius
sing moonbright wonders.

Yours is a language
of parables made classic
by love's sweet anguish.

The same hot lightning
that burns your blood with passion--
cools your fears with peace.

Angel of Gratitude

Each, shaped from a heart
divine — such is the nature
of your humble wings.

Love, Mercy, and Grace,
sisters all, attend your wounds
of silence and hope.

You are the good twin
and the bad. Not arrogant,
but jubilant...sweet...

With grief or without,
your flight commands awareness
of joy beyond pain.

Holy starbright of
endless heavens, for these tears —
truly — I thank you.

the bridge of silver wings

Feathers of Gold, Feathers of Silver

In July 2006, I sat down to write a short simple thank you note to fellow poets and writers who had graciously wished me well on my birthday. To my surprise, the intended short simple note came out of my pen in the form of the following poem:

ANGEL OF GRATITUDE

*Each, shaped from a heart
divine — such is the nature
of your humble wings.*

*Love, Mercy, and Grace,
sisters all, attend your wounds
of silence and hope.*

*You are the good twin
and the bad. Not arrogant,
but jubilant...sweet...*

*With grief or without,
your flight commands awareness
of joy beyond pain.*

Holy starbright of
infinite heavens, for these
tears--I do thank you.

Just the fact that it was a poem was the first big surprise.
The second was the style in which it was written, a
variation on the haiku that I had never used before. Had
my muse taken on the form of an angelic presence to gift
me with a unique way to say Thank You? Or had an
angelic presence paid me a visit to play the role of my
muse? I smiled at the possibilities, posted my Thank You
poem, and life went cautiously on about its modern-world
business.

So how astonished was I when another angel poem
materialized just a week later? Very! This one called itself
Angel of Grace. I don't recall a specific reason for its
composition, only afterwards feeling deeply inspired –
almost pressured in fact – to dedicate it to the English poet
Kate Burnside and her family. Since we have never met
nor even chatted, this dedication stunned Burnside at least
as much as it did me.

These angels of poetry, I thought, have a nicely wicked
and scary sense of humor.

Angel of Grace forced me to confront the possibility that
even though I had no intentions of writing additional
poems about the influence or presence of angels, some
additional poems might nevertheless have every intention
of making themselves known to me. It turned out they

74

did. Most were written down but some were not simply because I could not always hold the words or images long enough in my mind to do so. They would come in bursts of intense energy like exploding butterflies, dazzle me with their depth and light, then vanish.

The manner in which the poems continued to manifest intrigued me to no end. Predictably, the most violent among them was *Angel of War*. I did not like the concept of an *Angel of War* — probably because of the ongoing atrocities of the Iraq and Afghanistan wars — so tried to resist the act of physically writing a poem about one. This struggle not to pick up a pen and write clashed head-on with an intense compulsion to do exactly that. For more than a week I found myself engaged in this psychic battle. Any time I wrote a stanza in one notebook, just to get it out of my head, I would later write somewhere else a question challenging the nature of war. This tugging back and forth eventually gave the poem its final form of haiku-like stanzas followed by angry questions.

The *Angel of War* experience was a weird one that I did not have time to contemplate long because — talk about some serious irony — the next week the *Angel of Peace* showed up during a storm that knocked all the lights out. Every time I went feeling through the dark to do one thing, I would grab a candle or flashlight along with a pen and paper then stand wherever I was and write instead. Both *Angel of War* and *Angel of Peace* were featured in the July 2007 online issue of *Poetry Life and Times*.

By the time I wrote *The Poet-Angels Who Came to Dinner* , which turned out to be the thirteenth of the angel poems, in early 2007, I no longer had energy or room to doubt that I was involved in the creation of something at once singular and abstruse. The intensity of the writes continued to bug me a bit. Or maybe even a lot. Sometimes the words came like ecstatic utterances, sometimes like songs whispered from another time, like actual angelic possessions, or like mental files that had been downloaded while I slept and then printed via my pen as soon as I got up. I began to wonder how long they would go on.

As often happens when puzzled by something on the level of ordinary consciousness, the answer to my bafflement came on a higher level of dream consciousness. In what I described as a dream-vision, I saw dozens, or possibly hundreds, of angels above an ocean lined up across the sky in the form of an arc while I stood staring at them from the shores of a beach. The tops and tips of their wings glittered with the brilliance of silver starlight. The pulse and glow of this light seemed to hum a song that I was sure I had never heard before and yet that I recognized immediately, despite being unable to say what it was. Suddenly, the spirit of my father appeared beside me in the dream-- pretty much the way fathers are known to do. I asked him if all those angels lined up across the sky in the shape of an arc meant that I was going to write a lot more about angels?

"That's part of what it means," he said, then added, "but you're thinking too educated."

"Thinking too educated? How?" I noticed the silver of his hair was similar to that of the angels' wings and that his speech was more fluid than when he had lived in his world.

"You say they're forming an 'arc,' like something beautiful but not with practical purpose. They're really making a bridge. Wait a minute, that's not the way to put it either. They actually are a bridge. You only see the angels on one side of it. There're just as many on the other side. Now, Son, you know you ought'a recognize that bridge."

"Ummm, really, why should I?"

"Because you were born at the foot of it and you've been walkin' across it all your life. If it wasn't for all those silver wings spread out to help you on your journey, you would'a been dead or someplace screamin' in a nut house a long time ago."

"Well that makes sense. Why didn't you tell me this before you died?"

"It wasn't for me to tell. It was for you to make it to this point in your life so you could see it for yourself. That way you can't argue against it because the truth is a living part of you."

Before I could ask another question, I woke up.

In that soft haze between full consciousness and fading

dreams, I saw something else. There was my father standing on one bridge paved with feathers of gold; and there I was standing on another paved with feathers of silver. From where he stood, he smiled and waved. I woke up completely. Sitting up on the side of the bed, I grabbed the pen and notebook on my nightstand. Remembering the image of my father upon that bridge, I wondered if he had been a poet and never told me. Getting a better grip on my pen, I started writing.

Angel of Better Days to Come
(from *ELEMENTAL, The Power
of Illuminated Love*)

Rockets of blind faith
sputter and crackle dead dreams--
like time bleeding stars.

Through soft painted moans
a man watches his life drown
in waves of glass bones.

Celestial winds
blow chilled screams for love's mercy
down canyons of dread.

Through bright haunted smiles
a woman hums white magic--
sings pain into pearls.

Reflections of self
in multiple dimensions
whirl across the sky.

Machine guns fire knives

that slice the world's bloody tears
like bits of strange fruit.

Throbbing blue rhythms,
a torn heart wrestles naked
with wounds from the past.

Black holes coalesce
into mounds of burned feathers
and crucified trust.

Between death and hell
a bridge shining silver wings
offers his soul hope.

That good gardener,
who wept thorns plowing his fields--
harvests grace with joy.

Midnight Flight of the Poetry Angels
(in honor of a poet who became a president)

What once was blood streaks
your face with indigo tears
and lush midnight tunes.

Holding silver hands,
you compose a Tao of art
that heals broken wings.

Lips glow violet,
open to reveal tongues bright
with pearl metaphors.

A speckled halo
handcuffs the world's best liars
to soft dark passions.

Music's sweet labors
give birth to a springtime rush
of sighs rippling dreams.

Out of your mouth rhymes
blossom like warm paradigms
already in flight.

Golden, your songs,
nobly spinning planets on
their axis of love.

On faith's battered back
calm eyes etch prayers that cool
a nation's hot rage.

Inside these scarred hearts
genius flows incandescent
waves of truth made real.

Hope drowned in shadows
emerges fiercely splendid--
boldly angelic.

What Angels Call "A Poet"

"There I was without a face
and it touched me."
--Pablo Neruda

The dancing vortex of a sacred metaphor
swallows a man's blind broken heart,
impregnates the kidnapped soul of a woman,
crunches diamond skulls into whistling rivers
and splits the great womb of history
with days and nights of radiant progression.

Behind the raw hell of a screaming face
late spring blossoms a mask of emerald summers.
Tireless malice and courageous love claim their
    seasons.
A cosmic waterfall of antimatter pours and roars
nuclear destruction through cracks in one universe
as it floods another with songs of bright creation.

The dancing vortex of a sacred metaphor
clashes horns and halos to make wounded music
set to the tempo of a new era in brilliant labor.
Cyclonic flames spit bones of silver bells singing
with fresh-born souls sheathed in skins
    of quantum verbs,
and thus we see born what angels call--a poet.

Acknowledgments

It is true that poems generally have only a single name attached to them where authorship is concerned but in many ways poems are born of much more than any single individual. They evolve out of meetings of minds, the collective heartbeats of communities, and the shared journeys of similar souls. This book could almost have been titled *The River of Winged Voices* because much of my work in poetry has been a response to the voices of others presented through their poems, songs, movies, novels, plays, paintings, and other inspired works. It is my great honor to acknowledge as many as I can in this space at this time:

I remain grateful to the masterful painter Luther E. Vann for allowing the use of his art creation, "Angel of Mercy, Angel of Love," on the covers of previous editions of *The Bridge of Silver Wings* and for the inspired work presented in *ELEMENTAL, The Power of Illuminated Love.*
Since 2003, a fair number of my poems have first been introduced and critiqued by members of online literary communities. For their continued support and shared insights, I thank the members of: AuthorsDen, Blogit, Creative Thinkers International, GotPoetry.com, Red Room, *The Smoking Poet E-zine*, and The Writing Forum.

In addition, I am particularly honored to acknowledge the

publication of "There upon a Bough of Hope and Audacity" in the January 14-20, 2009 special edition of *The Savannah Tribune,* presented as a tribute both to the legacy of Dr. Martin Luther King, Jr., and the inauguration of President Barack H. Obama. I'm also pleased to note the featured presentation of my poem, "Notes for an Elegy in the Key of Michael," on the MJJ-777 website.

My gratitude as well to John Zeuli, whose amazing photography makes me look like many people's idea of a "real writer."

Last but never least: to all my readers and the inspiration they constantly provide through the gift of their shared passion for literature — Thank You.

Aberjhani

Made in the USA
San Bernardino, CA
23 August 2016